World's Greatest Sports Stars The World's Greatest Sports Stars
World's Greatest Sports Stars The World's
World's Greatest Sports stars The World's
World's Greatest Spor

Sports Illustrated KIDS

The World's Greatest

Soccer Players

by Matt Doeden

CAPSTONE PRESS
a capstone imprint

Sports Illustrated KIDS The World's Greatest Sports Stars is published by Capstone Press,
1710 Roe Crest Drive, North Mankato, Minnesota 56003.
www.capstonepub.com

Library of Congress Cataloging-in-Publication Data
Doeden, Matt.
    The world's greatest soccer players / by Matt Doeden.
    p. cm. — (Sports illustrated KIDS. the world's greatest sports stars)
    Includes bibliographical references and index.
    Summary: "Describes the achievements and career statistics of soccer's
greatest stars" — Provided by publisher.
    ISBN 978-1-4296-3925-5 (library binding)
    ISBN 978-1-4296-4870-7 (paperback)
    ISBN 978-1-4765-0194-9 (e-book)
    1. Soccer players — Biography — Juvenile literature. 2. Soccer
players — Rating of — Juvenile literaure. I. Title. II. Series.
GV942.7.A1D64 2010
796.334092'2 — dc22
[B]   2009028537

Editorial Credits
Aaron Sautter, editor; Tracy Davies, designer; Eric Gohl, media researcher;
    Laura Manthe, production specialist

Photo Credits
Corbis/EPA/Alberto Martin, cover
Dreamstime/Diademimages, 5 (left); Matt Trommer, 24; Santamaradona, 1 (left);
    Szirtesi, 4 (right)
Getty Images Inc./Claudio Villa, 18, 29; Kevork Djansezian, 23; Laurence Griffiths, 9;
    Simon Bruty, 17
Shutterstock/Ksash, backgrounds
Sports Illustrated/Bob Martin, 12; Bob Rosato, 1 (center), 14; Heinz Kluetmeier, 5 (right);
    Simon Bruty, 1 (right), 4–5 (background), 4 (left), 6, 11, 21, 27, 30–31 (background)

Statistics in this book are current through the 2011–12 season.

Printed in China by Nordica.
1212/CA21201636
122012
007062R

Table of Contents

Goal!

Smack! Lionel Messi kicks the ball at the open corner of the goal. Thump! Gigi Buffon makes a diving block to save the score. Soccer is the most popular sport in the world. From South America to Europe, fans go wild for their favorite teams. Soccer is filled with exciting action and strategy. Each game is a contest of skill and endurance. The sport's greatest players are truly global superstars.

thrilling **scores**   solid **defense**

athletic **moves**   amazing **goaltending**

Xavi Hernandez

Spanish soccer fans love to cheer for Xavi Hernandez, their country's most decorated player. The amazing passer has been called the best midfielder of modern times. His incredible skills helped Spain win the 2010 **FIFA** World Cup and the Euro 2008 and 2012 championships.

Name: Xavier Hernandez Creus
Born: January 25, 1980, in Barcelona, Spain
Height: 5 feet 6 inches
Weight: 150 pounds
Position: Midfielder

career League Statistics

Season	Team	Appearances	Goals
1998–1999	FC Barcelona	17	1
1999–2000	FC Barcelona	15	0
2000–2001	FC Barcelona	15	2
2001–2002	FC Barcelona	31	4
2002–2003	FC Barcelona	29	2
2003–2004	FC Barcelona	34	4
2004–2005	FC Barcelona	36	3
2005–2006	FC Barcelona	14	0
2006–2007	FC Barcelona	29	3
2007–2008	FC Barcelona	34	7
2008–2009	FC Barcelona	37	6
2009–2010	FC Barcelona	34	3
2010–2011	FC Barcelona	31	3
2011–2012	FC Barcelona	31	9
CAREER		**387**	**47**

achievements

UEFA European Championship: 2008, 2012
World Cup championship with Spain: 2010
Olympic silver medalist with Spain: 2000
World Soccer Player of the Year: 2010
UEFA Super Cup: 2010, 2012
UEFA Champions League: 2006, 2009, 2011

FIFA: Federation of International Football Association

fact

Xavi Hernandez was the first player to register assists in two Euro Cup finals. He helped Spain win Euro 2008 and Euro 2012 and became the most successful Spanish player ever.

Name: Steven George Gerrard
Born: May 30, 1980, in Whiston, England
Height: 6 feet 1 inch
Weight: 174 pounds
Position: Midfielder

career League Statistics

Season	Team	Appearances	Goals
1998–1999	Liverpool	12	0
1999–2000	Liverpool	29	1
2000–2001	Liverpool	33	7
2001–2002	Liverpool	28	3
2002–2003	Liverpool	34	5
2003–2004	Liverpool	34	4
2004–2005	Liverpool	30	7
2005–2006	Liverpool	32	10
2006–2007	Liverpool	36	7
2007–2008	Liverpool	34	11
2008–2009	Liverpool	31	16
2009–2010	Liverpool	33	9
2010–2011	Liverpool	21	4
2011–2012	Liverpool	18	5
CAREER		**405**	**89**

achievements

UEFA Euro Team of the Tournament: 2012
Captain of English national team: 2012
FWA Footballer of the Year: 2009
PFA Fans' Player of the Year: 2001, 2009
FA Cup Final Man of the Match: 2006
UEFA Club Footballer of the Year: 2005
FIFA Club World Championship Silver Ball: 2005
Led Liverpool to three Premier League titles

fact

Gerrard was England's leading scorer in the 2006 World Cup.

Steven Gerrard

There is little Steven Gerrard can't do with a soccer ball. The Liverpool striker can play anywhere on the field. He's a good attacker. But his strong running, tackling, and heading skills also make him a defensive star. Gerrard's abilities have made him one of the most valuable players in the sport.

personal information

Name: Franck Bilal Ribéry
Born: April 7, 1983, in Boulogne, France
Height: 5 feet 7 inches
Weight: 137 pounds
Position: Midfielder

career League statistics

Season	Team	Appearances	Goals
2001–2002	Boulogne	20	5
2002–2003	Alès	18	1
2003–2004	Stade Brestois	35	3
2004–2005	Metz	20	2
2004–2005	Galatasaray	14	0
2005–2006	Marseille	35	6
2006–2007	Marseille	25	5
2007–2008	Bayern Munich	28	11
2008–2009	Bayern Munich	25	9
2009–2010	Bayern Munich	19	4
2010–2011	Bayern Munich	25	7
2011–2012	Bayern Munich	32	12
CAREER		**296**	**65**

achievements

French Player of the Year: 2007, 2008
UEFA Team of the Year: 2008
German Footballer of the Year: 2008
World Cup, second place with France: 2006

fact

Ribéry was in a car accident at age 2. He has two long scars on his face from the accident.

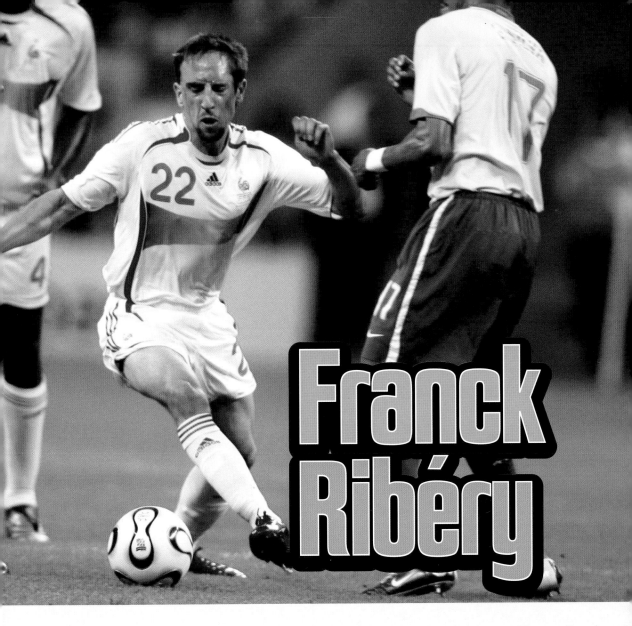

Franck Ribéry

Nobody hustles on the soccer field more than Franck Ribéry. He's often one of the smallest players on the field. But the midfielder makes up for it with his high-energy style. Ribéry is known as one of the game's best passers. When he's blocked in, he usually gets the ball to an open teammate. Many soccer fans consider him today's best French-born player.

Kaká

Many people feel Kaká is one of the best soccer players in the world. The Real Madrid midfielder, who goes by his childhood nickname, is the total package. He's big and strong, and he's often the hardest worker on any field. Kaká has amazing ball handling and shooting skills. He sets a great example for others with his hard work and **sportsmanship**.

Name: Ricardo Izecson dos Santos Leite
Born: April 22, 1982, in Brasília, Brazil
Height: 6 feet 1 inch
Weight: 161 pounds
Position: Midfielder

career League Statistics

Season	Team	Appearances	Goals
2001	São Paulo	22	12
2002	São Paulo	20	8
2003	São Paulo	10	2
2003–2004	Milan	25	10
2004–2005	Milan	33	7
2005–2006	Milan	28	14
2006–2007	Milan	30	8
2007–2008	Milan	30	15
2008–2009	Milan	31	16
2009–2010	Real Madrid	25	8
2010–2011	Real Madrid	14	7
2011–2012	Real Madrid	27	5
CAREER		**295**	**112**

achievements

FIFA World Player of the Year: 2007
IAAF Latin Sportsman of the Year: 2007
Named to 2008 *Time 100* as one of world's
    100 most influential people
UEFA Team of the Year: 2006, 2007, 2009
UEFA Champions League Top Scorer: 2007
World Cup championship with Brazil: 2002

sportsmanship: having respect for others and treating them fairly during a game

fact

At age 15, Kaká suffered a terrible spine injury in a swimming accident. Doctors feared he might never walk again. But Kaká made a full recovery.

Lionel Messi

Lionel Messi's **close control** skills and sharp vision make him the perfect striker. Messi is one of the smallest players in the game. But he uses his small size to his advantage. He can weave through traffic like no other player. And when it looks like he's cornered, he almost always finds an opening. As Barcelona's all-time top scorer, Messi is the best!

Name: Lionel Andrés Messi
Born: June 24, 1987, in Rosario, Argentina
Height: 5 feet 7 inches
Weight: 148 pounds
Position: Striker

Career League Statistics

Season	Team	Appearances	Goals
2004–2005	FC Barcelona	7	1
2005–2006	FC Barcelona	11	6
2006–2007	FC Barcelona	23	14
2007–2008	FC Barcelona	28	10
2008–2009	FC Barcelona	31	23
2009–2010	FC Barcelona	35	34
2010–2011	FC Barcelona	33	31
2011–2012	FC Barcelona	37	50
CAREER		**205**	**169**

achievements

FIFA World Player of the Year: 2009, and
    runner-up: 2007, 2008
FIFA Ballon d'Or: 2010, 2011
World Soccer Player of the Year: 2009, 2011
FIFPro World Young Player of the Year:
    2006, 2007, 2008
Argentina's Player of the Year: 2005, 2007
Captain of Arentina's national team: 2012
Olympic gold medal with Argentina: 2008

close control: to handle the ball near to one's own body

fact | Messi's nickname is *El Pulga,* or "The Flea."

personal information

Name: Cristiano Ronaldo dos Santos Aveiro
Born: February 5, 1985, in Funchal,
  Madeira, Portugal
Height: 6 feet 1 inch
Weight: 165 pounds
Position: Attacker

career League statistics

Season	Team	Appearances	Goals
2002–2003	Sporting CP	25	3
2003–2004	Manchester United	29	4
2004–2005	Manchester United	33	5
2005–2006	Manchester United	33	9
2006–2007	Manchester United	33	17
2007–2008	Manchester United	34	31
2008–2009	Manchester United	33	18
2009–2010	Real Madrid	29	26
2010–2011	Real Madrid	34	40
2011–2012	Real Madrid	38	46
CAREER		**321**	**199**

achievements

UEFA Euro Team of the Tournament: 2004, 2012
FIFA World Player of the Year: 2008
FIFA Ballon d'Or runner-up: 2011
UEFA Club Footballer of the Year: 2008
Captain of the Portuguese national team: 2012
Portuguese Footballer of the Year: 2007
World Cup, fourth place with Portugal: 2006
Champions League title with Manchester
  United: 2008

fact

Ronaldo's father named him after his favorite
actor, U.S. President Ronald Reagan.

Cristiano Ronaldo

Cristiano Ronaldo is always a huge scoring threat. He's a two-footed attacker, which means he can handle and shoot the ball with either foot. Ronaldo takes full advantage of his skills. He can attack from anywhere on the field. The 2008 FIFA World Player of the Year is one of the biggest stars in the game.

Gigi Buffon

No goalie controls a soccer game like Gigi Buffon. Soccer's greatest goalkeeper uses catlike reflexes to keep a **clean sheet**. Buffon's goaltending skills puzzle many opponents. They struggle to find an opening in his amazing defenses. During the 2006 World Cup, he had an incredible streak of 453 scoreless minutes. His great play helped Italy become a World Cup champion.

Name: Gianluigi Buffon
Born: January 28, 1978, in Carrara, Italy
Height: 6 feet 3 inches   Weight: 183 pounds
Position: Goalkeeper

career League Statistics

Season	Team	Appearances
1995–1996	Parma	9
1996–1997	Parma	27
1997–1998	Parma	32
1998–1999	Parma	34
1999–2000	Parma	32
2000–2001	Parma	34
2001–2002	Juventus	34
2002–2003	Juventus	32
2003–2004	Juventus	32
2004–2005	Juventus	37
2005–2006	Juventus	18
2006–2007	Juventus	37
2007–2008	Juventus	34
2008–2009	Juventus	23
2009–2010	Juventus	27
2010–2011	Juventus	16
2011–2012	Juventus	35
CAREER		**493**

achievements

Captain of the Italian national team: 2012
UEFA European Championship runner-up: 2012
UEFA Euro Team of the Tournament: 2008, 2012
Serie A Goalkeeper of the Year: 1999, 2001, 2002, 2003, 2005, 2006, 2008
European Footballer of the Year: 2006
World Cup championship with Italy: 2006
FIFA World Cup All-Star Team: 2006

clean sheet: when a goaltender does not allow the opposing team to score a goal

fact

Buffon comes from an athletic family. His mother was a discus thrower. His father was a weightlifter. And his grandfather's cousin was also a famous goalkeeper.

19

Name: Wayne Mark Rooney
Born: October 24, 1985, in Liverpool, England
Height: 5 feet 10 inches
Weight: 174 pounds
Position: Striker

career League Statistics

Season	Team	Appearances	Goals
2002–2003	Everton	33	6
2003–2004	Everton	34	9
2004–2005	Manchester United	30	11
2005–2006	Manchester United	36	16
2006–2007	Manchester United	34	14
2007–2008	Manchester United	27	12
2008–2009	Manchester United	30	12
2009–2010	Manchester United	32	26
2010–2011	Manchester United	28	11
2011–2012	Manchester United	34	27
CAREER		318	144

achievements

FWA Footballer of the Year: 2010
PFA Players' Player of the Year: 2010
FIFPro World Young Player of the Year: 2005
FIFA Club World Cup Golden Ball: 2008
First Team, FIFA Club World Cup: 2008
Sir Matt Busby Player of the Year: 2006, 2010
Champions League title with Manchester
    United: 2008

fact | During the 2004 UEFA Euro tournament, several experts called Rooney the best teenage player since the legendary Pelé.

Wayne Rooney

Few players can attack like England's Wayne Rooney. The Manchester United striker is a great goal scorer. Rooney got an early start to his career. He joined Everton's youth team at just 10 years old. And he played his first Premier League match at age 16. His aggressive style has helped him become one of England's best players.

Name: Fernando José Torres
Born: March 20, 1984, in Madrid, Spain
Height: 6 feet 1 inch
Weight: 172 pounds
Position: Striker

Career League Statistics

Season	Team	Appearances	Goals
2000–2001	Atlético Madrid	4	1
2001–2002	Atlético Madrid	36	6
2002–2003	Atlético Madrid	29	13
2003–2004	Atlético Madrid	35	19
2004–2005	Atlético Madrid	38	16
2005–2006	Atlético Madrid	36	13
2006–2007	Atlético Madrid	36	14
2007–2008	Liverpool	33	24
2008–2009	Liverpool	24	14
2009–2010	Liverpool	22	18
2010–2011	Liverpool	23	9
2010–2011	Cheslea	14	1
2011–2012	Chelsea	32	6
CAREER		**362**	**154**

achievements

FA Cup: 2012
UEFA Champions League: 2012
UEFA European Championship: 2008, 2012
UEFA Euro Golden Boot: 2012
World Cup championship with Spain: 2010
Pro Football Awards Team of the Year: 2008
UEFA Euro Team of the Tournament: 2008

fact

Torres' nickname is *El Niño*, which is Spanish for "The Kid."

Fernando Torres

Fernando Torres is a real force on the field. He's not afraid to take a shot. And this striker usually gets the goal. He became the faster player in Liverpool history to score 50 goals. His powerful shot also makes him a hero on Spain's national team. His team won the 2010 World Cup and the Euro 2012 tournament, where he scored three goals. What a champion!

Sergio Ramos

Sergio Ramos is a threat on both ends of the field. He's a strong, tireless defender. And his powerful **crosses** make him a force on offense. Ramos was a star of Spain's national team that won the 2010 World Cup. And his successful penalty shootout attempt helped boost Spain to the Euro 2012 championship.

Career League Statistics

Season	Team	Appearances	Goals
2003–2004	Sevilla	7	0
2004–2005	Sevilla	31	2
2005–2006	Sevilla	1	0
2005–2006	Real Madrid	33	4
2006–2007	Real Madrid	33	5
2007–2008	Real Madrid	33	5
2008–2009	Real Madrid	32	4
2009–2010	Real Madrid	33	4
2010–2011	Real Madrid	31	3
2011–2012	Real Madrid	34	3
CAREER		**268**	**30**

achievements

UEFA European Championship: 2008, 2012
UEFA Euro Team of the Tournament: 2012
World Cup championship with Spain: 2010
FIFA World Cup All-Star Team: 2010
UEFA All-World Defensive Player of the
    Year: 2006
UEFA Team of the Year: 2008
FIFA.com Team of the Year: 2008

cross: a long pass to a teammate across the width of the field

fact

While growing up, Ramos dreamed of becoming a bullfighter. But he was always sad to see the bull die at the end of a fight.

personal information

Name: John George Terry
Born: December 7, 1980, in London, England
Height: 6 feet 1 inch
Weight: 180 pounds
Position: Center Back

Career League Statistics

Season	Team	Appearances	Goals
1998–1999	Chelsea	2	0
1999–2000	Chelsea	4	0
1999–2000	Nottingham Forest	6	0
2000–2001	Chelsea	22	1
2001–2002	Chelsea	33	1
2002–2003	Chelsea	20	3
2003–2004	Chelsea	33	2
2004–2005	Chelsea	36	3
2005–2006	Chelsea	36	4
2006–2007	Chelsea	28	1
2007–2008	Chelsea	23	1
2008–2009	Chelsea	35	1
2009–2010	Chelsea	37	2
2010–2011	Chelsea	33	3
2011–2012	Chelsea	31	6
CAREER		**379**	**28**

achievements

FA Cup Champion: 2000, 2007, 2009, 2010, 2012
UEFA Champions League: 2012
FIFA World Cup All-Star Team: 2006
Chelsea Player of the Year: 2001, 2006
Pro Football Awards Player of the Year: 2005
UEFA Club Defender of the Year: 2005, 2008, 2009
Premier League Champion: 2005, 2006, 2010

fact | Terry joined Chelsea's youth program at age 14. He's been with the club ever since.

John Terry

Center back John Terry is a goalkeeper's best friend. His ability to block opponents and steal the ball make him one of the game's best defenders. Terry is a smart player and captain of the Chelsea team. Terry's amazing skills helped Chelsea win England's Premier League three times.

Name: Samuel Eto'o Fils
Born: March 10, 1981, in Nkon, Cameroon
Height: 5 feet 10 inches   Weight: 165 pounds
Position: Striker

Career League Statistics

Season	Team	Appearances	Goals
1997–1998	CD Leganés	28	3
1998–1999	Real Madrid	1	0
1999–2000	Real Madrid	2	0
1999–2000	Real Mallorca	9	6
2000–2001	Real Mallorca	25	11
2001–2002	Real Mallorca	29	6
2002–2003	Real Mallorca	29	14
2003–2004	Real Mallorca	32	17
2004–2005	FC Barcelona	37	25
2005–2006	FC Barcelona	34	27
2006–2007	FC Barcelona	19	11
2007–2008	FC Barcelona	18	16
2008–2009	FC Barcelona	36	30
2009–2010	Internazionale	32	12
2010–2011	Internazionale	35	21
2011–2012	Anzhi Makhachkala	22	13
CAREER		**388**	**212**

achievements

Captain of Cameroon national team: 2012
FIFA World Cup Golden Ball: 2010
Olympic gold medalist with Cameroon: 2000
African Player of the Year: 2003, 2004, 2005, 2010
Top scorer in the African Cup of Nations: 2006, 2008
UEFA Champions League Best Forward: 2006
UEFA Team of the Year: 2005, 2006

fact

Eto'o was the youngest player to participate in the 1998 World Cup. He was just 17 years old.

Samuel Eto'o

Cameroon's Samuel Eto'o is one of the greatest African soccer players of all time. The award-winning striker uses blazing speed and an accurate shot to attack defenses. His amazing skills have helped him score dozens of goals during his career. He is also a big part of Cameroon's national team. He led Cameroon to an Olympic gold medal in 2000.

Glossary

clean sheet (KLEEN SHEET) — when a goaltender doesn't allow the opposing team to score any goals in a game

close control (KLOHSS kuhn-TROHL) — to keep a soccer ball near to the body and under control, especially when defenders are nearby

cross (KRAWS) — a long pass to a teammate across the width of the field

endurance (en-DUR-enss) — the ability to keep doing an activity for long periods of time

sportsmanship (SPORTS-muhn-ship) — fair and respectful behavior toward others when playing a sport

strategy (STRAT-uh-jee) — a plan for achieving a goal

World Cup (WURLD CUP) — a competition held every four years in which national soccer teams from around the world compete against each other for the title of world champion

International Soccer Organizations

FIFA — the Fédération Internationale de Football Association (French for Federation of International Football Association); FIFA oversees international soccer competition, including the World Cup

IAAF — the International Association of Athletics Federations, which governs a wide range of international athetics, including soccer

Premier League — a professional soccer league in England

UEFA — the Union of European Football Associations; the UEFA governs soccer in Europe

Read More

Adamson, Heather. *The Best of Pro Soccer.* Best of Pro Sports. Mankato, Minn.: Capstone Press, 2010.

Buckley, James. *Soccer Superstars.* Boys Rock! Chanhassen, Minn.: Child's World, 2007.

Shea, Therese. *Soccer Stars.* Sports Stars. New York: Children's Press, 2007.

Internet Sites

FactHound offers a safe, fun way to find Internet sites related to this book. All of the sites on FactHound have been researched by our staff.

Here's all you do:

Visit *www.facthound.com*

FactHound will fetch the best sites for you!

Index